I'M
LIL RAT,
THE WRITER
&
ILLUSTRATOR

DATS
B|ZZZLE
AKA BRENNEN
AKA MY CO-ILLUSTRATOR

! ♡ playing my music loud. i ♡ ANIMALS and nature and TREASURE HUNTS!

I LUV MY
RAT PAK

2 my FAMILY & BECAUSTIES
for holding my heart

for the LIL KID
inside us all.

MK·B

HAPPY sounds the best. except

i'M LIL RAT (Katie's inner kid) u CAN CALL
ME DAT. I ♡ TO PLAY, DRAW & WRITE. I like

FIND

ANIMALZ
LIL RAT
WORDZ

WHERE
WINNIE WUZ
P RUNEZ
BAND-AIDZ

FROM PAIN

TALK ABOUT
ONEZ YOU DON'T
UNDERSTAND ♡

2 PASSION
4
PuRPoSE
(GIVE LOVE)

2 PEN

these words and drawings paint my heart
and are a reflection of the river of love
that flows through us all

Dear Reader,

I've had all kinds of off days in my life: relaxing ones, sick ones, scary ones, sad ones, angry ones, adventurous ones, magical ones, ones i thought might never end. But no matter how off days felt, I always had unshakable faith things would get better. That my heart would turn back on, that rips would mend and I'd love and be loved again. This book is a just pass to that unshakable faith.

On the off days I thought might never end, 2 things got me through: flowers and water. flowers brought me back to the beauty of the present moment, to my sacred senses, to the magic of God's creation. Water helped me remember that even though blue is my favorite color, I can expand my palette beyond the pain. And beyond the pain, i can connect to Purpose: Remembering the Truth that I am a child of God worthy of Love no matter what. Just like flowers, there is Beauty and Love pumping through us that can brighten someone's day.

It can feel hard sometimes to remember that Truth when your heart hurts and your mind is stormy. But, those moments are opportunities to lace Love where it was lost. They are also opportunities to be Creative about weaving Wonder into places your instinct is to worry. Off Days is my gift to you to do just that and a lil more... To pause. to connect to the lil kid inside of you. to breathe in peace and release the Beast. To reset, not regress. To Water the Soil of your Soul. To remember your Heart is a garden and it's ready to Bloom. To connect to the Love inside of you. Enjoy ♡ Happy Reading! i Love you. ♡ MKB (mary kathryn Bruzzone.)

Off Days: Finding the On Button

Copyright © 2025 Katie Bruzzone

Book Design by Zoe Mellors

ISBN: 979-8-89694-602-1 (Paperback) | ISBN: 979-8-89694-603-8 (Hardcover) | ISBN: 979-8-89694-601-4 (eBook)

First edition 2025

OFF DAYS

FINDING THE ♥N BUTTON

Katie Bruzzone

Ally woke up on the WRONG side of the bed.

She tried everything, but nothing felt right.

The room was too COLD.
The food was too HOT.
The show was too LOUD.
The bed was too HARD.
The blankets were too SOFT.

She was having an OFF day, and it seemed like NOTHING could turn her heart back on, at least not today.

"What's WROOOOONG with today?"

Ally howled.

"Go AWAY! Don't come back another day!"

Then something magical happened.
Ally could barely believe her eyes.

"Nothing is wrong with you, Ally,"
said the otter.

"You're having an OFF day.
We all have OFF days sometimes."

"What's an OFF day?"

Ally asked.

"Will it ever turn back ON?"

"Of course it will,"

said the otter.

"Can I show you how?"

The otter began to flow...

"Little did you know, I've been listening all along.
Your roars, tears, and tantrums
made my beastie powers strong!

I learned to understand the things you feel but can't say.
And now I'm here to guide you through emotional play!"

"I'm your emotional partner in crime,
and when you feel ANGER, it is a sign."

"When the pain you feel inside is something you can't hide,
you turn to anger to protect a cut that's since dried."

"Anger shows up in all kinds of ways.
Some days, a phrase sets things ablaze.
A groan, a tone, ready to explode.
It blurts, alerts, converts, and diverts
attention away from all that hurts."

"Ouch!
It hurts!

My heart HURTS,"

Ally cried.

"I'm SCARED of this place, and I want to hide."

"What do you NEED?
What can I do?"
asked the otter.

"Hug me. Cuddle me,"
said Ally.
"Help me stay connected to you.
Harmonize with my tune.
Tell me it will be better soon.
Feel the pain in my heart,
and don't hurt me anymore too."

"It sounds like you're SAD."

The lion perked up into view.

"Sadness feels loss, a disconnection from love.
Like something is missing, and your heart is unplugged,"
said the lion.

"We can plug you back in!
We can answer the call.

The call to adventure is inside of you.

What feels blue?
Let's find a clue."

"What's blue leads to water in places you withdrew.
That water helps seeds grow in the dark parts
of you and me, too."

"I have seeds in me?"

Ally asked.

"Yes!"

roared the lion.

"Your heart is a garden. It's ready to bloom."

"Pick a flower to hold you when you feel blue.
That flower is your on-button, the plug to love inside of you.
It's a place for your heart to shine through.
It's the clue, tried and true,"
said the otter and the lion.

"Now you know how feelings flow.
With a beastie breath,"
said the otter.
"Easy come, easy go."

"And don't forget flowers!"

said Ally.

"They have powers too!
They remind me that how I feel is okay,
and the bad feelings are not here to stay.
I don't need to wish away an off day.

Because guess what?"

"Love is here to stay.

Flowers lead the way ..."

"And the beasties
are ready to play!"

I spent so much of my life resisting Off Days and growing through pain. Some of it was healthy and helped me become a D1 athlete, innovator and artist. Some of it was unhealthy and hurt me in ways it took years to understand and feel to heal. I felt lost and lonely. Like no one would understand the darkness storming my mind. Like my heart might ache forever. But I'm here to show you it doesn't last forever. There is salvation. There is Redemption. Any block you face, YOU CAN break through. And there's a purpose in that process: it p the pathway to your Soul. Each trial clears and charts the trail through the forests, valleys and caves of your being. Each tear leads to treasure. The art blooming out of your Seat Of Unconditional Love whispers and whimpers through your Wonders and wounds. So lean in and listen close.

This book is my Redemption story. A lil window into my Soul so you can feel into yours. Its my invitation to you to explore it, to know it deeply, to live from it so you can live the life of your Dreams.

There is a tune, texture, tone and combination of Superpowers only you can gift this world. And you watering those Sacred seeds in the Soil of your Soul. and gifting them to the world is how we awaken the new Golden Age.

To do this, you must honor your heart and have unshakable faith in yourself and humanity and the magic of Nature. Let Jung ("Young") at Heart echo through you when pain or fear strikes and let it teach you a lesson in Love. Let this book be your on button whenever things feel off. Let this book remind you Off Days are opportunities to water your Sacred seeds. Let this book inspire your Infinite Potential. Nothing is impossible. Take the next right step. i Love you ♡ JK.3

ABOUT THE WRITER

Katie Bruzzone is a leadership coach, innovation consultant, inspirational speaker, facilitator, artist, and writer on a mission to unleash creative genius and develop the Jung ("Young") at Heart. She offers products and services that build confidence, creativity, and mastery in all ages.

A student of life and weaver of worlds, Katie is devoted to reviving an unwavering spirit that cultivates holistic health and a passion for learning. Her specialty is finding inspired and effective ways to implement innovative strategies that help individuals, families, and organizations grow and excel. Katie is a former collegiate athlete, a graduate of the Haas School of Business at UC Berkeley, and a Master of Science in Strategic Design and Management from Parsons School of Design.

Connect with Katie

CONTACT: https://www.katiebruzzone.com/book/online

WEBSITE: https://katiebruzzone.com

EMAIL: bruzzonekatie@gmail.com

INSTAGRAM: https://www.instagram.com/katiebruzzone/

LINKEDIN: https//www.linkedin.com/in/katie-bruzzone/